Leonardo da Vinci

By Iain Zaczek

WAYLAND

WAYLAND

This edition published in 2014 by Wayland

Copyright © 2014 Brown Bear Books Ltd.

Wayland
Hachette Children's Books
338 Euston Road
London NW1 3BH

Wayland Australia
Level 17/207 Kent Street
Sydney, NSW 2000

All Rights Reserved.

Brown Bear Books Ltd.
First Floor
9–17 St. Albans Place
London
N1 0NX

Author: Iain Zaczek
Managing Editor: Tim Cooke
Designer and artwork: Supriya Sahai
Picture Manager: Sophie Mortimer
Design Manager: Keith Davis
Editorial director: Lindsey Lowe
Children's publisher: Anne O'Daly

ISBN–13: 978-0-7502-8461-5

Printed in China

10 9 8 7 6 5 4 3 2 1

Wayland is a division of Hachette Children's Books,
an Hachette UK company.
www.hachette.co.uk

Picture credits
Key: b = bottom, bgr = background, c = centre, is = insert, l = left, mtg = montage, r = right, t = top.

Special thanks to The Art Archive
Front Cover, ©The Art Archive/Musee d'Orsay, Paris/Collection Dagli Orti; 4, ©Thinkstock/photos.com; 5, ©Shutterstock; 6t, ©Thinkstock/Claudio Divizia; 6b, ©Thinkstock/Claudio Divizia; 7, ©Thinkstock /Assawin; 8, ©Public Domain/Uffizi; 9t, ©Public Domain/Louvre, 9b, ©Shutterstock /Maksim Budnikov; 10, ©Thinkstock/Janaka Maharage Dharmasena; 11, ©The Art Archive/Musee d'Orsay, Paris/Collection Dagli Orti; 12-13, ©The Art Archive/Galleria Degli Uffizi, Florence/Mondadori Portfolio/Electa; 15, ©The Art Archive/National Gallery of Washington; 17, ©The Art Archive/DeA Picture Library; 19, ©The Art Archive/Czartorysky Museum, Cracow; 20-21, ©The Art Archive/Mondadori Portfolio/Electa; 23, ©The Art Archive/Musee d'Orsay, Paris/Collection Dagli Orti; 25, ©The Art Archive/Musee du Louvre, Paris/Collection Dagli Orti; 26, ©The Art Archive/Pinacoteca di Brera, Milan/Mondadori Portfolio/Electa; 27, ©The Art Archive/Vatican Museums, Vatican City/Mondadori Portfolio/Electa.

All artwork: © Brown Bear Books

Brown Bear Books has made every attempt to contact the copyright holder. If you have any information please contact licensing@brownbearbooks.co.uk

Contents

Life story

Leonardo da Vinci is one of the most well-known artists in history. He died over 500 years ago, but his paintings are still famous today.

Leonardo da Vinci was born on 15 April, 1452, in Tuscany, in northwest Italy. We do not know much about his childhood. He was probably born in the town of Vinci, from which he took his name. He was the son of a lawyer named Piero da Vinci. His mother was a peasant girl named Caterina. Leonardo had 11 half-brothers and sisters, but most of them were born long after him. He grew up as an only child.

Birth name: **Leonardo di Ser Piero da Vinci**

Born: **15 April, 1452, Vinci, Italy**

Died: **2 May, 1519, Amboise, France**

Nationality: **Italian**

Field: **Painting**

Movement: **High Renaissance**

Influenced by: **Andrea del Verrocchio**

Self-portrait
by Leonardo, 1512

VINCI was a small village in the hills of Tuscany. It was near Florence, the region's capital city.

Leonardo was clever and eager to learn about things. He did not have a good education, but he was good at maths and music, and at drawing.

Art apprentice

When Leonardo was about 15, his father sent him to be an apprentice pupil to Andrea del Verrocchio. Verrocchio was one of the leading artists in the city of Florence. He was a goldsmith and sculptor, as well as a painter. Leonardo learned about art by working in Verrocchio's studio.

Famous Paintings:
- 🌲 **The Annunciation** 1472–75
- 🌲 **Portrait of Ginevra de' Benci** 1474–78
- 🌲 **The Virgin of the Rocks** 1483–86
- 🌲 **Lady with an Ermine** 1489-90
- 🌲 **The Last Supper** 1495–98
- 🌲 **Mona Lisa** 1503–17
- 🌲 **The Virgin and Child with Saint Anne** 1508–1515

'The knowledge of all things is possible.'

Unfinished painting

In 1472, when Leonardo was about 20, he finished his apprenticeship with Verrocchio. He was now called a master painter. This meant he could have opened his own studio, but he kept working with Verrocchio until 1481. Leonardo's first big job came when he was asked to paint a large picture to hang behind the altar in a monastery near Florence. Leonardo never finished the picture, but he had painted enough of it to show the world what a great artist he was.

Moving city

Leonardo did not finish the painting because he had moved from Florence to the city of Milan, in the north of Italy. There he worked for the ruler of the city, Duke Ludovico Sforza. For the next 20 years, Leonard worked for the duke as an artist. He also became a military expert and an engineer. Leonardo liked to find out about how things worked. He was interested in invention. Leonardo designed many weapons for the Duke, although none were ever made.

OLD MILAN Leonardo worked in the city for over 20 years as an artist and an inventor.

HELICOPTER Leonardo drew a diagram of this spinning flying machine in his sketchbook.

ART CENTRE
Florence was an important city in the late 15th century. Its rulers gave work to many artists and architects.

Large-scale works

Ludovico asked Leonardo to make two huge works of art. One was a statue of Ludovico's father on a horse. Leonardo made a large clay model of the statue, but once again never got around to making the statue itself. He was too busy with other things.

The other work for Ludovico was a wall painting, or mural, in a monastery. Leonardo painted *The Last Supper.* This is one of his most famous paintings. People thought it was a masterpiece. But Leonardo had used a new kind of paint for the picture. It was a disaster. A few years later, the paint started to peel off the wall.

Important people

Andrea del Verrocchio – artist and teacher

Duke Ludovico Sforza – patron

Cesare Borgia – patron

Leo X – pope

Francis I – king and patron

'Details make perfection, and perfection is not a detail.'

THE RENAISSANCE

Leonardo lived during a period known as the Renaissance. People in Italy studied the ideas of the ancient Romans and Greeks. 'Renaissance' is a French word meaning 'rebirth'. People thought they were bringing back the old ideas from ancient times.

The Renaissance lasted from the 14th to the 17th centuries. Leonardo, Michelangelo and Raphael were the leaders of what became known as the High Renaissance in the 16th century. They had important patrons. Pope Leo X gave Raphael and Michelangelo work. Raphael painted the Pope's portrait (above).

Back to Florence

In 1499 the French army invaded Milan. The Duke was forced to leave. Leonardo returned to Florence. He began to work for Cesare Borgia. Borgia was from a powerful family. His father was Pope Alexander VI. Leonardo designed weapons for Cesare Borgia. He also drew detailed maps for him. In about 1503 Leonardo started painting his most famous picture, the *Mona Lisa*.

Moving around

In 1506 Leonardo returned to Milan, where he stayed until 1513. When more fighting broke out near Milan, he moved to Rome. He asked the new pope, Leo X, for work, but the Pope was more interested in giving his support to younger artists, such as Michelangelo and Raphael.

There are three classes of people. Those who see. Those who see when they are shown. Those who do not see.

Francis I asked Leonardo to join his court. Leonardo was now famous not only for painting but also for being full of ideas on many subjects.

Final home in France

Leonardo was so famous that many other people wanted him to work for them. The French king, Francis I, invited Leonardo to move to France. Leonardo moved to a large house near Francis' castle at Amboise, in northern France, not far from Paris. Francis enjoyed talking to Leonardo about science and physics, as well as about art. He believed that Leonardo was a genius.

Leonardo died at Cloux, near Amboise, on 2 May, 1519. He was 67. No one knows where he was buried.

Francis had a castle at Amboise, outside Paris. He gave Leonardo a large house nearby, where the artist spent his final years.

How Leonardo painted

Leonardo was always looking for ways to make his paintings seem more real.

In the past, many artists had painted scenes that did not look very real. They did not have much detail and lacked movement. Leonardo was fascinated by everything he saw. He studied the smallest details. He sketched ordinary things over and over, until he could draw them perfectly.

Realism

Leonardo studied the world around him very carefully. He made detailed drawings of details like rocks, plants and the human body. That made them look more realistic when he included them in paintings.

Study of a Man's Neck
Leonardo da Vinci (c.1510)

Leonardo learned about the bodies of people and animals. That helped him draw them in a realistic way. He drew muscles in a way that made it look as though people were moving. He also drew accurate flowers, fabrics and rock formations.

Leonardo used a technique called *sfumato*. His colours are carefully blended into one another. There are no lines between them.

Mona Lisa (detail)
Leonardo da Vinci (c.1503–17)

Leonardo was one of the first Italian artists to use oil paints. They were quite a new invention. Oil paint dried slowly. That meant Leonardo could work very carefully. He built up his pictures with many thin layers of paint. It is impossible to see where one colour changes into another. This technique is called *sfumato*, which is Italian for 'like smoke'. Leonardo said that he painted 'without lines or borders, in the manner of smoke'.

The Annunciation

This is one of Leonardo's first masterpieces. He painted it in the early 1470s, at the end of his apprenticeship with Andrea del Verrocchio.

The painting shows an important story from the New Testament of the Bible. The archangel Gabriel is telling Mary that God has chosen her to be the mother of Jesus. 'Annunciation' means 'announcement'.

DA VINCI'S

Palette of the picture

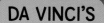

In the Frame

🌿 The original painting of *The Annunciation* is 98 cm (39 inches) tall and 217 cm (85 inches) wide.

🌿 Very little is known about the early history of this picture. It was discovered in a convent near Florence.

Leonardo was fascinated by the natural world. The angel's wings are based on those of a bird.

Leonardo has painted the Annunciation taking place in Italy. These types of trees grow in the Italian countryside.

Gabriel holds a long-stemmed lily in his left hand. This flower is always linked with Mary. It was meant to show that she was a good person.

The Church celebrates the Annunciation in March, in the spring. Leonardo has included spring flowers in this painting.

Portrait of Ginevra de' Benci

Leonardo painted this portrait between 1474 and 1478. Leonardo was in his early 20s. He was still working in Verrocchio's studio.

Ginevra came from a rich family in Florence. She was about 16 when Leonardo painted her. The portrait might have been painted to celebrate her engagement to be married. Although Leonardo was so young, he changed the way artists painted portraits. He tried to show a person's character from the expression he painted on their faces.

Ginevra's hair looks almost real. Leonardo said that curly hair was like flowing water.

In the Frame

❧ The original painting of Ginevra de' Benci is 38 cm (15 inches) tall and 37 cm (14.5 inches) wide.

❧ Leonardo used his fingers to dab paint on in some places. His fingerprints can still be seen on the picture surface.

DA VINCI'S
Palette of the picture

Where the spirit does not work with the hand, there is no art.

Ginevra looks directly at us. Most Italian artists of the time liked to paint people from the side.

Leonardo loved word games. These are the leaves of a juniper bush. The Italian word for 'juniper' is *ginepro*, which is like 'Ginevra'.

In Italy, portraits were usually done indoors. Leonardo painted Ginevra as if she was standing outdoors.

The Virgin of the Rocks

Leonardo painted this picture between 1483 and 1486. He was hired to paint it for the Church of San Francesco in Milan, Italy. It was meant to be the central panel of a large altarpiece.

The altarpiece also included sculptures and side-panels that showed angels playing musical instruments. Leonardo's painting shows Christ, Mary his mother and an angel meeting a very young John the Baptist. The meeting takes place in a strange, imaginary landscape.

In the Frame

♥ The original painting of *The Virgin of the Rocks* is 199 cm (78.3 inches) tall and 122 cm (48 inches) wide.

♥ Leonardo made two nearly identical paintings of this subject. This one is in the National Gallery, London, UK; the other is in the Louvre in Paris, France.

DA VINCI'S

Palette of the picture

This child has a long cross made of reeds. Leonardo's audience would have known this was a sign that he was John the Baptist, the patron saint of Florence.

The angel's hand is only a sketch. Leonardo often left details unfinished in his paintings.

Christ's fingers are raised. This shows he is blessing the viewer. In religious paintings like this, everything has a meaning.

This plant is called Star of Bethlehem. It is a symbol, or sign, of the Virgin Mary.

Lady with an Ermine

This is one of Leonardo's most beautiful portraits. He painted it in 1489–90. At the time he was working for Ludovico Sforza, the Duke of Milan.

The young woman in the picture is Cecilia Gallerani. She was a girlfriend of the Duke. The ermine is a white stoat. Leonardo included it because it had a special meaning for Cecilia and the Duke. It was a word play on the name Gallerani, because *galé* is Greek for 'ermine'. The Duke had also been awarded a special honour called the Order of the Ermine. Cecilia was famous for writing poetry.

DA VINCI'S

Palette of the picture

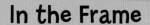

In the Frame

🦡 The original painting *Lady with an Ermine* is 54 cm (21 inches) tall and 39 cm (15 inches) across.

🦡 The painting was taken from Italy to Poland in the 18th century.

Cecilia's hand is slightly too large. Leonardo may have based it on one of his detailed sketches.

The artist sees what others only catch a glimpse of.

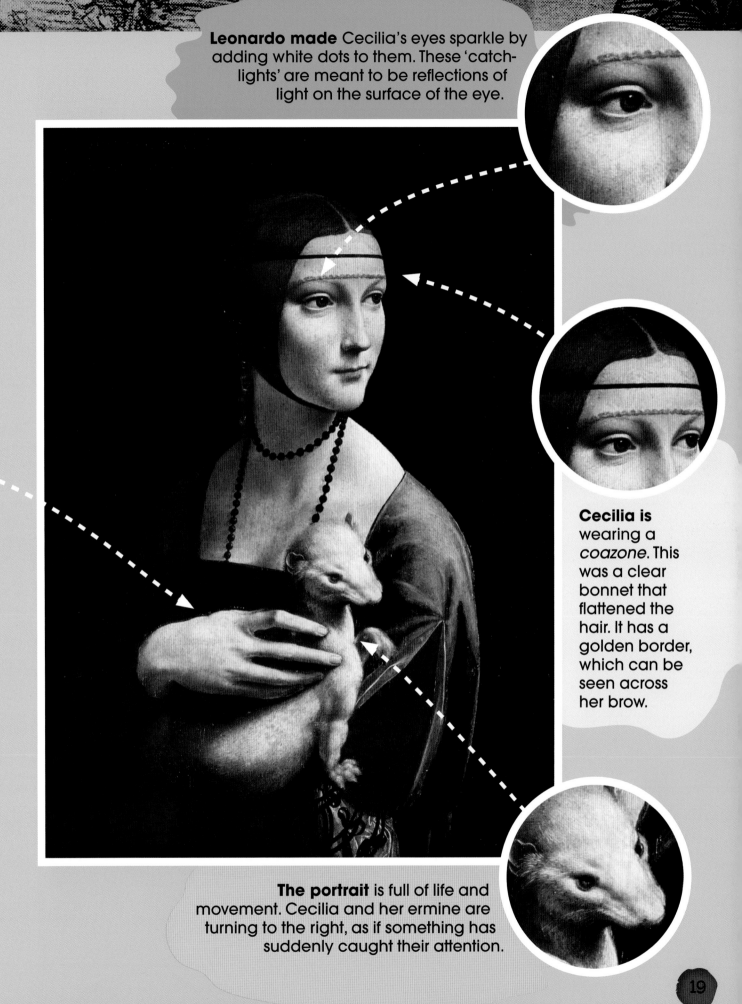

Leonardo made Cecilia's eyes sparkle by adding white dots to them. These 'catch-lights' are meant to be reflections of light on the surface of the eye.

Cecilia is wearing a *coazone*. This was a clear bonnet that flattened the hair. It has a golden border, which can be seen across her brow.

The portrait is full of life and movement. Cecilia and her ermine are turning to the right, as if something has suddenly caught their attention.

19

The Last Supper

Leonardo painted this huge mural on the wall of the dining room at the monastery of Santa Maria della Grazie in Milan. It was painted between 1494 and 1498.

In this picture Christ has just told his disciples that one of them will betray him to the Romans. Leonardo shows the men's reactions to this shocking news. Usually, artists had to paint murals quickly while the plaster on the wall was still wet. Leonardo liked to paint slowly. He invented his own way of painting on walls, but soon after he finished this painting, it began to peel off. The mural has been restored several times since then.

DA VINCI'S

Palette of the picture

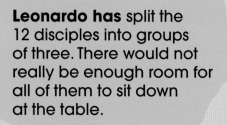

Leonardo has split the 12 disciples into groups of three. There would not really be enough room for all of them to sit down at the table.

Christ sits in the centre of the picture and wears colourful clothes. His head is framed by the bright light of the largest window. This sets him apart from the others.

In the Frame

🔹 The original painting of *The Last Supper* is 460 cm (181 inches) tall and 880 cm (346 inches) wide.

🔹 The painting was restored in a 20-year project from 1978 to 1999.

Judas is painted leaning away from Jesus. He holds the purse of silver that he received for betraying Christ.

The light falls on the same wall as in the real dining room. The monastery's main windows are to the left of the painting.

Mona Lisa

This is the most famous portrait in the world. It is also the most mysterious. It was started between 1503 and 1506, but Leonardo may have worked on it until 1517.

Lisa's left eye gazes directly at the viewer, but her right eye looks slightly to one side. This makes it seem as if her eyes are following you as you move in front of the painting.

The woman is probably Lisa Gherardini. Lisa was the wife of a wealthy merchant from Florence. 'Mona' is a title. It is short for 'madonna', or 'my lady'. However, we do not know for sure who the woman was or why the portrait was painted. The picture is famous because she has a mysterious smile.

This smile made the *Mona Lisa* famous. For centuries people have tried to guess what she is thinking. Leonardo knew how every muscle in the face worked, so he painted expressions very carefully.

In the Frame

🖤 The original painting of *Mona Lisa* is 77 cm (30 inches) tall and 53 cm (21 inches) wide.

🖤 Leonardo kept the painting. He took it when he moved to France, where it was later bought by King Francis I.

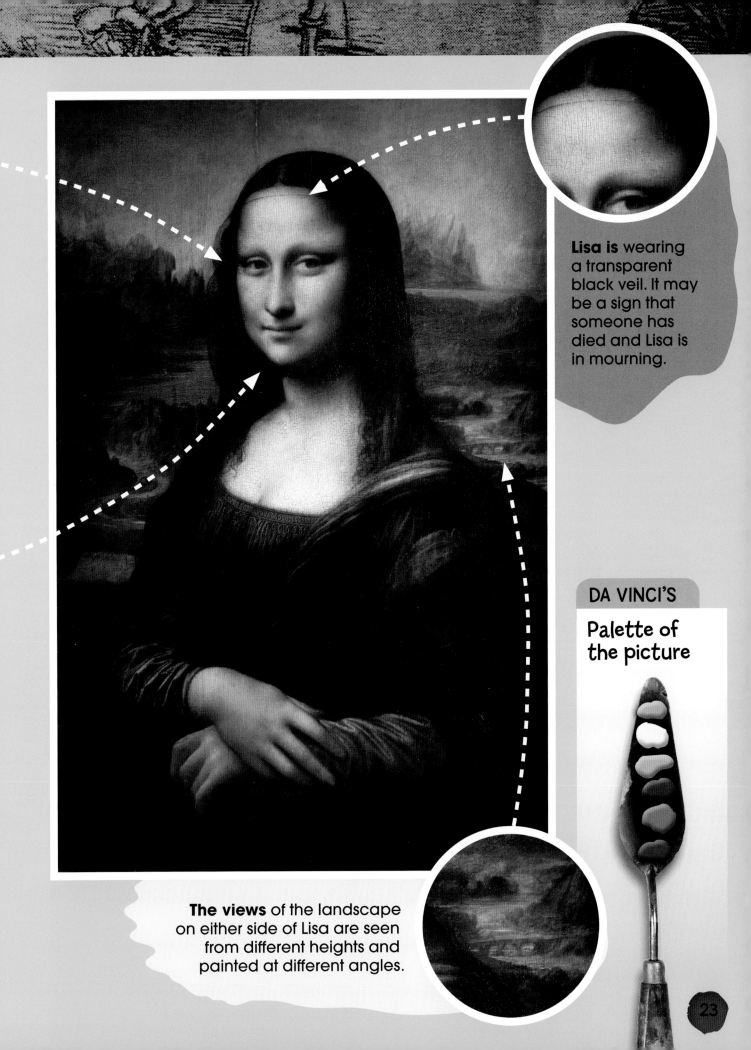

Lisa is wearing a transparent black veil. It may be a sign that someone has died and Lisa is in mourning.

DA VINCI'S

Palette of the picture

The views of the landscape on either side of Lisa are seen from different heights and painted at different angles.

The Virgin and Child with Saint Anne

Leonardo started this oil painting of the Holy Family in around 1508. It shows the baby Jesus with his mother, Mary, and Mary's mother, Saint Anne.

Leonardo started several pictures of this subject. This one was probably painted for King Louis XII of France. He may have wanted it to celebrate the birth of his daughter. The subject was suitable. The king's wife was called Anne. As usual Leonardo worked slowly. The king died in 1515, before the painting was finished.

Mary is sitting on her mother's knee. In Leonardo's century, this was the way artists showed that Anne, Mary and Jesus were related.

In the Frame

The original painting of *The Virgin and Child with Saint Anne* is 168 cm (66 inches) tall and 112 cm (44 inches) wide.

Leonardo made a large sketch for a similar painting to include John the Baptist, but it was never finished.

There is a cliff or ravine between us and the people. This and the mountain background are signs that the scene is taking place in heaven.

The mountains in the background look unreal. Artists often showed distant mountains by using blue and gray colours.

This lamb is a symbol of Christ. Jesus was often described as being 'the Lamb of God'.

DA VINCI'S

Palette of the picture

What came next?

Leonardo only completed a few paintings, but they were important. He influenced the work of two younger painters, Raphael and Michelangelo. They were the three greatest painters of the 16th century.

Leonardo changed how artists painted portraits and religious scenes. In his portraits he did not just try to show what someone looked like. He painted movement and expression to make his subjects look more alive. His pictures of scenes in the Bible were very dramatic.

RAPHAEL'S SCENE is full of movement. Look at the man bending the rod on the right.

Raphael
The Marriage of the Virgin, 1504.

Leonardo also changed what people thought about artists. In the past, they had been treated like any other craftsmen. Artists were highly trained and skilled, but people did not think they were very clever. Leonardo changed that. He was a remarkable thinker. As well as being a painter, he was also a brilliant scientist, engineer, inventor and architect.

Leonardo wrote down many of his ideas about art. That meant people could read about them long after his death. From the 17th to the 19th centuries, Leonardo's book *Treatise on Painting* was widely used in art schools to help train new generations of artists.

THIS IS A DETAIL from Michelangelo's painting on the ceiling of the Sistine Chapel in Rome.

Michelangelo
God Creates Adam
1508–12.

Renaissance painters

- Michelangelo
- Raphael
- Titian
- Giorgione
- Correggio
- Fra Bartolommeo

How to paint like Leonardo

It is difficult to paint exactly like Leonardo. He was one of the most brilliant artists ever to have lived, but he did many creative things besides painting. Try these for yourself.

WHAT YOU'LL NEED:

- a mirror
- paper
- pencils
- eraser
- pens

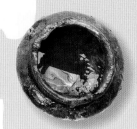

1.

Leonardo had lots of ideas for inventions. But he liked to keep them secret. One way he did this was by using mirror writing. He wrote his notes backwards, so they could only be read in a mirror.

2.

Rest the edge of a mirror on the left-hand side of your paper. Starting in the top righthand corner try writing a message by copying what you see in the mirror. Your words will be back to front, so they should go from right to left as you write them. Be warned: It feels very strange to begin with! Start with a pencil so you can erase letters if you make a mistake.

3.

Try coming up with your own inventions. One of Leonardo's most famous inventions was a flying machine. Use a new sheet of paper to design your own flying machine (or another machine). Draw the parts as clearly as possible. Use your mirror to label the different parts of the drawing in mirror writing.

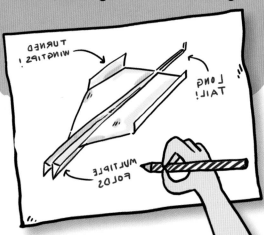

4.

Now show your drawing to your family or friends. See if they can figure out what the writing says. Use your mirror to show them.

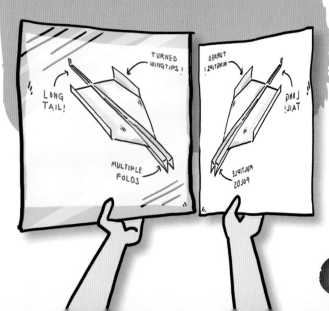

Timeline

1452: Born in Vinci, Italy.

c.1467: Apprenticed to Andrea del Verrocchio in Florence.

1472: Becomes a master painter.

1481: Starts painting an altarpiece, which is never finished.

1482: Moves to Milan to work for Duke Ludovico Sforza.

c.1495: Begins painting *The Last Supper*.

1499: Leaves Milan when the French invade and returns to Florence.

1506: Returns to Milan.

1513: Moves to Rome but does not find much work.

c.1516: Moves to France.

1519: Dies near Amboise, France.

Glossary

altarpiece: A religious painting made to hang behind the altar in a chuch.

apprenticeship: A period when someone learns a trade by working as an apprentice, or pupil, for someone skilled.

master painter: An artist who has completed his apprenticeship and is qualified to open his own studio.

masterpiece: A work of art that displays great skill by the artist.

mural: A painting that is painted directly onto a wall.

palette: The range of colours an artist uses in a particular painting.

panel: A wooden section of a larger painting, such as an altarpiece.

patron: Someone who pays an artist to work for them.

realistic: Something that looks true to life.

Renaissance: A period when artists in Italy and other parts of Europe tried to make art based on the ideas of the civilizations of ancient Greece and Rome.

sketch: A drawing that is often done before painting a picture.

studio: A place where an artist paints.

traditional: Something that has been done in the same way for a long time.

Further information

BOOKS

Edwards, Roberta. *Who Was Leonardo da Vinci?* Grosset and Dunlap, 2005.

Nardo, Don. *Leonardo da Vinci* (Eye on Art). Lucent Books, 2012.

Nichols, Catherine. *Leonardo da Vinci* (The Primary Source Library of Famous Artists). PowerKids Press, 2006.

Romei, Francesca. *Leonardo da Vinci* (Art Masters). The Oliver Press, 2008.

Strom, Laura Layton. *Leonardo Da Vinci: Artist and Scientist* (Shockwave: Life Stories). Children's Press, 2007.

Tello, Antonio. *Leonardo da Vinci* (My Name Is). Turtleback, 2006.

Tracy, Kathleen. *Leonardo da Vinci* (Art Profiles for Kids). Mitchell Lane Publishers, 2008.

MUSEUMS

You can see Leonardo's famous paintings from this book in these museums:

The Annunciation
Uffizi Gallery, Florence, Italy.

Portrait of Ginevra de' Benci
National Gallery of Art, Washington, DC, USA.

The Virgin of the Rocks
Louvre Museum, Paris, France AND National Gallery, London, UK.

Lady with an Ermine
Czartoryski Museum, Krakow, Poland.

The Last Supper
Santa Maria della Grazie, Milan, Italy.

Mona Lisa
Louvre Museum, Paris, France.

The Virgin and Child with Saint Anne
Louvre Museum, Paris, France.

WEBSITES

www.bbc.co.uk/history/historic_figures/da_vinci_leonardo.shtml
BBC biography of Leonardo.

makingartfun.com/htm/f-maf-art-library/leonardo-da-vinci-biography.htm
'Meet Leonardo da Vinci' page from Art Library, with links to projects.

www.sciencekids.co.nz/sciencefacts/scientists/leonardodavinci.html
Fun facts from Science Kids focusing on Leonardo's inventions.

www.ducksters.com/biography/leonardo_da_vinci.php
An introduction to Leonardo from the Ducksters website, with fascinating facts.

Publisher's note to educators and parents: Our editors have carefully reviewed these websites to ensure that they are suitable for students. Many websites change frequently, however, and we cannot guarantee that a site's future contents will continue to meet our high standards of quality and educational value. Be advised that students should be closely supervised whenever they access the Internet.

Index